FIRST

DRAFT

OF A

MAN

QUILLKEEPERS PRESS

ISBN: 978-1-969601-04-0

Published by Quillkeepers Press, LLC
PO Box 10236
Casa Grande, AZ 85130

Featured Poems

X Marks the Spot

My new notebook is freaking me out,

pages so crisp and unblemished.

My unruly scrawl would surely ruin them.

My pen rests between my fingers,

but it's cold in my flat

and writing is uncomfortable.

Under my desk there's a plastic storage container

with all my old notebooks inside.

If anyone were to rifle through them, they'd find:

every goodbye to Dad,

every time Mum let me down,

every friend I misjudged,

every girl who didn't like me, and

my extensive archive of unsaid words.

Pondering these memories gets the blood

circulating in my hands again.

In an effort to reclaim some ambition,

I draw myself a treasure map,

grab a pair of scissors and cut

a circular version out of the page.

It'll do for now.

I blue-tack it to the wall

and stare at it.

Pratfalls

I'm not dead

but the life I'm living isn't mine.

Lost myself in 4am party kitchens

and surrounded myself with people

I don't care about.

It's easier.

Can't be angry at nothing.

Can't be disappointed by nothing.

Can't fail if I'm not trying in the first place.

I never lowered my white flag,

just tore it up to make bandages

and bound them too tightly around my arms.

At some point,

I'll have to feel it again: the torso hollowing,

the short, sharp shock.

That sinking feeling

when the floor gives way.

I'm Not This Miserable, I Swear

It's delicate, fiddly, and ultimately self-defeating

to fish a buried wick from gloopy dregs.

My depression doesn't keep me in bed anymore.

It's more like being trapped in a glass box.

My mind is

a butter knife,

and I can't finish my dinner.

Making rollies gives me

something to do besides fidget,

besides feel. Then occasionally

life will snap me out of my taciturn safety.

I'll see two calves playing together

or meet a nice girl.

Fleeting moments have always comforted me.

The problem is,

when my heart is mostly a purely functional pump

that's a lot of pressure to put

on the thing with the nice girl.

And the calves.

The Fool

An analytical eye glared

from behind pretty girly makeup.

She surveyed like a predator

and killed like one.

She bit me by the scruff

and dangled me above my body issues.

Let me run away,

then caught me again,

dragging me across the ground of my awkwardness.

Am I the fool, the willing victim?

To enter her territory willingly

when I knew exactly who she was?

Surface

Give me a seaweed crown to wear.

I cannot sing above the ground.

Muted vowels, gurgled notes,

froth and chant a taunting round.

Pledges born in dull flint dawns

evaporate in silent dusks.

Visions of the rising tide

eroded by Atlantic gusts.

Breached the surface where I found

airs and graces tightly wound.

Would that I could swim unbound,

ghost in a shipwreck, or king of the Merpeople.

Give me a seaweed crown to wear.

I cannot sing above the ground.

Mind the Gap

I dodged the fare on the train to Dream Junction

and forgot to get off. This carriage is my coffin,

trundling along as the scenery flits past.

I palm my hand on the window

and remove it again.

The route is intimately familiar.

It kisses my lips like it's fallen out of love with me.

Alone,

I settle for the enervate embrace

as my tentative lurches of faith in myself

inevitably fizzle out

like my handprint on the glass,

dissolved by condensation.

Five years lost in the mist

left me bloated with notions,

but it was a phantom pregnancy.

Coal

Black stain on candleglass.

Lingering scent of lime and basil,

just about detectable.

Wick caked in remnant wax.

Dust of crumbled grate.

A fire lit by the shy boy

who abhorred all he became.

In futile attempts to cleanse his soul

he's scorched off his fingerprints,

and seared his vocal folds.

The crooked welt beneath his nose

occupies the halfspace between coping

and capitulating.

Sestina of Self-Esteem

I sent my self-help workbook back

'cause I still don't have any self-esteem.

They said I can't have a refund

because I'm a piece of shit.

The last condom in my wallet is hope,

not buying another box is realism.

There is no grey within my realism.

I cannot get lost fragments back,

the ones I held in high esteem.

What I can do is try to refund

the notions that have gone to shit.

A master alchemist I'll be, I hope.

There is always, perplexingly, hope,

harshly disciplined by realism.

I try to write myself some self-esteem,

but my lovemaking is shit.

Handwriting always leans back,

contrary etchings demand refund.

In attempts to replenish the fund,

the depleting resources of hope

gather dust around the back,

a time-worn layer of realism.

And maybe I would give a shit

if I had some self-esteem.

Solitude seeks external esteem

rather than an internal refund.

Better to embrace realism,

something that actually ignites hope.

Maybe it's something I should back

instead of waiting for that shit.

Life can be shit,

subject to ever-shifting esteem,

the ensuing maiming of hope,

and sloppy sutures of realism.

But where is my damn refund?

I still want my money back.

I gave the workbook to charity in hope

someone could be a second-hand shit,

a condom inflated by realism.

Moths

I'd love to roll her up and smoke her,

be that high.

But I couldn't even skin up,

prune-fingered from stewing in her grandiosity.

Those weren't butterflies in my stomach,

but moths,

when she'd visit my flat in The Old Forge

to gorge on my undivided attention.

Once, parting outside the Horse and Hound,

I looked back over my shoulder,

but didn't spot her.

Later, she said she'd seen this...

while making sure I was looking back.

There weren't enough eyes in the world

to gaze upon her,

and I was one of many flapping around her flame.

Eventually,

the tonnage of her self-reverence

drove me into the ground.

Once she was done terrorising everyone in town,

she fled to Lisbon

to drink Ginjinhas and be philosophical and profound

and post selfies with identical men,

while I sit

in my shit Skibbereen flat,

writing about her.

The Time I Bailed on Valentine's Day
to Write a Poem

That love was a famine road, cruel and futile.

Absent wood or steel, I clawed at rocks.

Built in circles, or nowhere at all.

Sick, absent sustenance, I toiled for scraps

until, haggard, I sagged in some godforsaken ditch

to sleep for years.

When I woke, I buried my heart there

and traipsed the sprawling backroads home.

My gait was lighter and heavier than before.

Each haunted, wayward footfall

a beat further out of step with past serenades,

as the echoes sewed myears shut.

On the hushed pilgrimage,

I chiselled a resilient foundation.

No longer sinking my fingernails

into the gravel of another's hubris.

Painstaking, seemingly aimless, I laid my path.

Eventually, my face surfaced.

Though I still swallow the rubble

so I can choke on it.

Is it chronic?

My lethargy, my begrudgement.

The idea of romance was beaten out of me.

Still, I must not be dead if I miss it.

Woodwork

I don't have a mechanical mind,

so I dropped woodwork as soon as I could.

First year was alright, mostly easy stuff.

There was a sanding machine in the back of the
workshop,

sandpaper wrapped around a whizzing wheel.

We whittled edges off timber lumps until they were smooth,

resinous wood vapour filled our nostrils.

Not being up to much woodworking,

I took my sweet time with the sanding tasks.

And the filing, polishing.

Loneliness is a sanding belt.

The longer you spend pressed to the grit,

the smoother you become, the glossier your voice.

An indistinguishable lump.

Eventually, you start copping out.

Running down dead ends you know are dead ends,

going on defensive dates.

Blowing kisses at scarecrows.

Then, when it doesn't work out,

you can say you didn't care anyway.

And succumb to solitude's seduction,

the gaping embrace of cold blue screen lights.

A ghost's hand on your shoulder.

'*Hello*'.

Vulnerability

The thought of it makes my anus clench

as if runny fragility might trickle down my leg.

And I'm doing it again.

Showing everybody how *clever and funny* I am.

I used to be a sensitive little boy who cried all the time.

Somehow, without anybody explicitly telling me to,

I learned to muzzle myself.

Do you ever hide something to keep it safe,

but then you can't find it again?

I can't pinpoint why or when I shed my humanity.

Mummified in advance of death and

it's not like somebody is going to stumble upon my tomb.

So, I'll have to unfurl the linen myself,

strand by strand, thread by thread,

like winding an old clock backwards.

Navigating Life

It starts off with little pricks. I ignored those,

cruised along a slipstream of blind young eyes.

Before long, my skin was riddled with holes.

Punctured sails drift, then capsize.

I braced against the hailstone pelt—

heartbreak failure betrayal—

To withstand engulfing gales

I had to be clinker-built.

The map I bought was a deception,

so I made wild overcorrections

of ego, excess, and faux-amity.

Wound up choked by regret and apathy.

Downcast eyes miss beacon beams,

hiding foes beneath the surface,

and the ones lurking in my cyclic themes.

Returning to their worn-out circus.

I drank and fumed and pissed and scowled

to run from my lack of composure.

Self-hatred was much cosier

than the world I disavowed.

I can't pretend to end with hopeful platitudes,

as I tend to self-abuse.

The climb will be long, the climb will be hard,

and I'm here, at the start.

Close

With people, mostly

I feel like a horse in a man costume.

With you close to me,

the horse remembers how to gallop.

If happiness can be defined,

it might just be laughing in the sunshine

while we drink bottles of Rossini,

and emo tunes blared from the Anker Soundcore speaker.

We're both... lonely. Cooler than crowds.

But there's no pretence in our magnetism.

Let's rest stacked in each other's limbs

and never come down from this hormonal dizziness.

When you wake dishevelled, face drained of
complexion,

hair rumpled, palms sweaty,

I spot myself studying you

like you are a magical creature.

And I know.

The Other Man

I love you and it is awful.

Butterflies dance in my sinking gut

to the tune of recurrent folly.

You need me and it is pressing.

Your endless demands and grasping hands

validate me, but when you free my windpipe,

grim reality fills my lungs.

You're my number one hit, but I'm your B-side.

Still, I remain at your convenience

while feigning deafness towards the bum notes.

The rhythm is familiar, I keep playing along

to a beat with no hook.

Almost Love

My throat no longer croaks out bromides.

The shared story is dead, trounced by the self.

I'm tired of almost love stories.

My eyes no longer linger on relics.

The purest of feelings look strange now, too earnest.

I'm tired of abortive love.

My tongue no longer puckers up to flatter falsehoods.

Sincerity lags behind us, an injured thing we won't
slow down for.

I'm tired of abhorrent love.

My ears reject the noise of temporary forevers.

Authenticity has been mugged by performance.

I'm tired of caricatured love.

My hands no longer cling to fractured people.

There's too many pieces of them to hold.

We're so insecure, so unsure of ourselves,

we don't even try.

I'm tired,

tired,

tired.

Shutdown

Whenever I think I've shorn my shell, I look down.

It's intact.

My flexible, retractable straitjacket.

The romance between melancholic solitude and I is dead

We're waiting for the right time to leave,

but we love each other, and we're comfortable together.

Idioms are bullshit,

misery doesn't love company, she's loyal.

My irises are exclamation marks,

drooping from constant vigilance.

I never investigate another's

in case I see their fallibility,

their humanity, or mine.

In case they see I'm a stumped,

love-hungover-fuck-up,

whose body remembers his estrangement.

I'll never leave my neck exposed again.

Past blunders crawling around my ear make me wince.

The bumbling half-thoughts poorly expressed

from one so eloquent on paper.

Holiday Shampoo Smell

Hell smells like OGX collagen shampoo,

the one I always got at Dublin airport

'cause I thought it was fancy.

Coconut milk clings to the back of my neck,

creeping up to my ears whispering *'chump'*.

I barely remember when she hijacked my life,

but she hijacked it well.

Kidnapped me from the Lock Bar one night and next thing,

I'm the other man, in love, and I can't say,

and we're in Budapest and she's shouting at me

about tobacco

and everything else,

and years passed and we could never confront it,

no matter how many times we stayed up 'til 4am.

It was all I could do to nurse my raw udders

and sulk commendably,

but I couldn't pretend hard enough

that I didn't love her to believe it,

to not come running.

Stupid naïve, lonely puppy boy

with my broken little heart.

She swindled me a closeness that was smoke.

Then she bailed, and I despise her for it.

But I love her,

and I'd still sell my soul

for five minutes of her attention.

I'm so *stuck*.

Mired in her steep denial ditch,

marinating in the torment of questions,

as if the answers aren't clear.

Stupid naïve lonely puppy boy

with my broken little heart.

Thirty-Two

Growing up is hard and boring.

Hard and boring.

Hard and boring.

It looked like I celebrated my birthday.

Lunch with friends on Saturday,

a date on Sunday.

Sounds great, except I didn't feel like celebrating.

The lunch was purely so I could say I did something,

and my date is now backing off ominously.

Kieran's just out of hospital, couldn't drink.

Liz couldn't get a babysitter.

At least Claire hung around until my bus

so I could have a second beer.

I'm sick of cokeheads, so didn't want anything mental.

But a little fun would've been nice.

What the hell do you do when you're thirty-two

and no longer being mental?

Something hard to organise that's just boring.

My date was kind, interesting,

tall, Greek, smokes like me.

We overlapped at UL.

None of this stopped it being awkward.

I suppose she didn't like me.

Suppose that's how it goes.

Meeting people is so difficult,

and the rejection barely stings these days.

Hard and boring.

By Tuesday, there's nowhere to hide.

It's my birthday and my parents are gone

and I'm by myself.

So I break my streak, get stoned

and tuck into a chocolate cake I bought myself.

Hard and boring.

Hard and boring.

Hard and boring.

Ghosted

Before undressing, I check if she's replied.

A first burst, and the shower head stutters.

The stream recedes, spluttering like a sick child.

On the bus to town,

I spot the treetops of Lough Hyne

poking through the fog.

The longest she's gone without messaging.

The nettles wavering in the breeze distract me

before I consider the unthinkable,

another double text.

No. She might still be busy. Just go to Aldi.

The Ukrainians bunch together at the bus stop,

always first in line,

standing precisely where the door will hiss open.

They've never missed it but, I suppose

they're understandably nervous.

We've been talking for a month. I squeeze in.

Once home, the sun makes a noble effort

to brighten my mood,

but I find the heat stifling.

Bananas in the fruit bowl, mince in the fridge.

We half planned to hike around Goleen this weekend.

I don't get it. She always seemed so polite.

A week of silence.

Time to strim the grass.

Boiled Mince

He whistles when he moves

because the hole goes right through him.

He stuffed it with the rags of who he used to be,

but that didn't fill it.

He has a heart like boiled mince.

He cooks the flavourless lump

with his friends who aren't his friends,

gnaws on the chewy rump,

regurgitates it for the perverted chicks.

He realises emptiness need not be heavy,

it can float, light and airy,

like scented candles and an open window.

And though his better angels visibly bristled

when he danced on the strings of devils,

he learned to hear those whistles

with a fresh pair of ears.

Momentum

Wind blows, and dead skin sprinkles the ground

as it falls from my face.

Shedding, moulting.

Lighter, lighter.

The abrupt draft burst open the locked doors.

Freer, freer.

Rusty hinges ripen into spokes

and a wheel has been fashioned

of the doors.

Rounder, rounder.

Spinning freely, seeking upward gravity

to utilize as my own jazz

rather than lose my grasp

like water swallowing my ears.

Tether, tether.

A self-portrait in reverse,

unable to relinquish

but from ash it can be resurrected.

Higher, higher.

The Builder

A cute cottage window light beckons from an
evening's distance.

White nestled in green, like it grew out of the hills

with its homely, misshapen quirks.

The longer I walk towards it, the more the road
sprawls.

The milk teeth trail I left has long washed away.

Only forward now.

Why tread followers' footsteps when the path is solitary?

Pick a spot,

stop,

and build.

A Man Now

Do you remember the earliest decisions

you ever made about yourself?

I was twelve

at Wimbledon market.

Bought a little skull and bones ornament

with the word 'BOLLOCKS' emblazoned on it.

Sick.

I thought I was a man.

I wasn't.

Or at sixteen.

In the Patrick Street Penney's in Cork,

clothes shopping with my own money.

Walked out with two pairs of jeans.

One gray, one black

because I was a rocker.

I thought they made me look like a man.

They didn't.

Or my last two years of school,

swapping the park for the pub.

Four beers and a naggin of vodka,

behaving like an idiot.

I thought that's what men did.

It isn't.

Or at college,

smoking outside before class.

Wearing big jackets and swearing all the time.

I thought I was a wise man.

I wasn't.

When I got my first job and first flat,

I so badly wanted to do things I was too shy for
before.

Hanging out with pretty (awful) girls,

convincing myself I really liked raves.

I thought I was a cool man.

I wasn't.

I remember burying my father

in a suit too big for me,

feeling indoctrinated somehow.

I must be a man now.

Nearly.

I remember burying my mother

and not fearing the day.

Delivering the eulogy

and not worrying about the crowd.

I've loved, I've lost.

I've smashed it and I have fucked it.

Been broke, been loaded.

Been kicked out of my flat.

Had my heart broken.

Been up in court.

And I've been sacked.

My life has gone tits up more times than I can count

and I've been alright every time.

I can go out

and not have to prove anything,

not even speak if I don't want to

I can go for a run dressed up

just like my favourite football man!

Because I want to.

I can tell the pretty girl she's awful

and to leave me alone,

if that's what suits me.

I can cut people off.

I can cook, I can find work.

I can spend money or I can save it.

I can take care of my damn self, by myself.

Through everything,

I've grown into a more confident person

than I ever thought I could be,

and I feel conflicted about this.

Because had I realised sooner

I might've capitalised.

But whatever I did or didn't do,

at this point I can say

with a reasonable degree of certainty;

I'm a man now,

and d'you know what?

You can all go fuck yourselves.

Connor Lynch is an emerging poet who was originally inspired to write by Patrick Kavanagh, whose work explores the beauty of rural places. As someone who grew up in West Cork, Ireland, this naturally appealed to him. However, thankfully, he has since broadened his writing beyond pure imitation. With a background in journalism, a lifelong love of poetry, and a current career in content writing, he has always pursued writing in one form or another. He writes poetry on themes of grief, legacy, identity, mental health, love, politics, and nature. Connor was a 2025 recipient of a Munster Literature Center bursary for a mentorship in poetry. His poems have been featured in *FullStop UL*, the *Azarão Lit Journal*, and *Sunday Mornings at the River*. When he isn't writing, Connor spends time taking care of his dog, watching football, and photographing the beautiful scenery around where he lives.